What Should I Write?

Birthday Wishes,
Sympathy Sentiments,
Get Well Messages,
Congratulations,
Mother's & Father's Day
Greetings

Madeleine Mayfair

What Should I Write? Birthday Wishes, Sympathy Sentiments, Get Well Messages, Congratulations, Mother's and Father's Day Greetings
© 2016 Madeleine Mayfair

Cover design © 2016 Madeleine Mayfair
Images copyright Rawich, feelart, gubgib, Victor Habbick
Courtesy of Freedigitalphotos.net

ISBN-13: 978-1523888795
ISBN-10: 1523888792

TABLE OF CONTENTS

What Should I Write?

101 Birthday Wishes for Greeting Cards

Madeleine Mayfair

Do you freeze up every time a birthday card gets passed around the office? Everybody else seems to know exactly what to write, and you can't just sign your name. What do you do?

Consult this book!

It contains 101 unique sentiments you can scrawl on birthday cards for friends, family, co-workers, or even that special someone in your life—everything from The Basics to Silly, from Thoughtful to Casual. There's even a Lovey-Dovey section! No matter whose birthday card crosses your path, you'll be able to handle it no sweat.

Kick your fear of "Blank Inside" cards to the curb. Or put your artistic skills to use and make your own! No need to worry about what you'll write inside.

You can conquer any card with "What Should I Write? 101 Birthday Wishes for Greeting Cards."

THE BASICS

1. Best wishes for a wonderful year!
2. Happy birthday to a very special YOU!
3. May the coming year be the best one yet!
4. Wishing you a very happy day and a delightful year ahead!
5. May this birthday greeting bring you every kind of joy!
6. Thinking of you on your birthday.

7. Here's hoping your birthday is everything you want it to be!

8. Today's your day. Enjoy it!

9. Fond birthday wishes for a magical year ahead!

10. May all your birthday wishes come true!

11. It's your birthday. Have a blast!

12. Wishing you a very happy birthday.

13. May your birthday bring you every kind of joy!

14. Hope you have a fun-filled birthday!

15. Best wishes for a birthday that holds one surprise after another.

16. Happy Birthday to a friend I can always count on.

17. Wishing you the brightest birthday cheer.

18. Heartfelt birthday wishes for a very special someone!

19. It's been too long! Hope to see you soon, and have a very happy birthday!

20. May your birthday bring you extra special excitement!

CASUAL

21. Do you realize how incredibly amazing you are? Well, I do! Happy Birthday!

22. We all appreciate how much you do for us throughout the year. Have a wonderful birthday—you deserve it!

23. Your birthday is a perfect time to celebrate your successes. Ya done good, kid!

24. Happy Birthday! May the year ahead build on all your great achievements.

25. If you ever forget how cool we think you are, just pick up this card and you'll remember. We think you're the best!

26. Warm wishes for a birthday that's filled with laughter and love!

27. When was the last time you took a day just for yourself? Well, your birthday is the perfect opportunity to do just that. Have a good one!

28. Here's hoping your birthday is as perfect as any day could possibly be!

29. Have a cupcake or two, or five. Hey, it's your birthday—you deserve a little sugar!

30. Wishing you all the joy your heart can handle on your big day. Have a good one!

31. Here's to your special day and all the wonder in the world!

32. Wishing you all the best that life has to offer… on your birthday and all year long!

33. May all your birthday's joyful moments stay with you throughout the year.

34. Have a big slice of cake and a huge glass of wine. Live it up on your birthday!

35. A toast to you on your happy day! May the whole year sparkle like champagne!

36. Someone as amazing as you deserves a birthday full of freedom, joy, and excitement. Have a good one!

37. Wishing you all kinds of pleasure and cheer… today, tomorrow, and all through the year!

38. It's your day. Take the reins, hold on tight, and party 'til you drop!

39. Happy Birthday to you! Here's hoping you get everything your heart desires.

40. You deserve a day that's devoted just to you. Have a wonderful birthday!

41. May the warmth and happiness that begins on your birthday last all year. This is your day. Enjoy it!

THOUGHTFUL

42. Sending all my best and fondest wishes to you on this momentous day. A very happy birthday to you, my dearest friend!

43. Happy Birthday to the person who's always there when I need a shoulder to cry on, a hand to hold, or simply a special friend to laugh with.

44. I know you say you're not a "birthday person," but your birthday means a lot to me because YOU mean a lot to me. Enjoy your special day!

45. Your birthday doesn't just mark the day you were born, it commemorates your very existence. And I'm so glad you exist, because my life just wouldn't be the same if you weren't in it.

46. I've never met anyone quite as selfless and considerate as you. I can't even hope to compete, so I'll only say Happy Birthday! I appreciate your thoughtfulness more than you'll ever know.

47. May this birthday fill your heart with love, joy, and everything that's wonderful in life!

48. Wishing you a beautiful, bouncing, bountiful birthday and a very happy year ahead!

49. Here's hoping every moment of your special day reminds you how many people care about you. Have a very happy birthday!

50. I know we haven't kept in contact as much as we could or should, but I want you to know you're often in my thoughts and always in my heart. If you ever need someone to talk to, here I am, wishing you a very happy birthday and a wonderful year.

51. Warm birthday wishes can make your heart feel toasty even on the coldest winter night. Happy Birthday to a warm-hearted winter baby and a wonderful friend!

52. Your birthday is the perfect opportunity to indulge in something sweet, to dream of greatness to come, and to open your heart to the best life has to offer. Enjoy this day devoted to YOU!

53. May you hold sunshine in your heart through all life's rainy days.

54. Today's a day that's yours alone, to do whatever your heart desires. Here's hoping your birthday brings you everything you could ever wish for!

55. Caring birthday thoughts for someone who's always ready to appreciate life's little wonders.

56. May today's happy moments burn bright throughout the year. Have a delightful birthday!

57. Even the most mundane experiences can remind an attentive soul that grace and beauty reside everywhere in life. May your birthday reveal love, laughter, and deep meanings that will live in your heart all year round.

58. I know it's been a rough year and you've faced some incredible turmoil, but I hope the love your friends show you on your birthday shines like a beacon to guide you through life's darker days.

59. If I could make one wish for you, I really don't know how I'd choose. Happy days or peaceful years? Perfect health or incredible wealth?

Maybe I'll start by wishing you a very happy birthday, and sincerely hope all the rest will follow.

60. You deserve every success and good fortune life has to offer. May all your fondest dreams come true! My warmest birthday wishes to you!

61. I sincerely hope your birthday brings you every special moment your secret heart desires. If anybody deserves a wonderful day, it's you. Happy Birthday!

SILLY

62. Nothing says "Happy Birthday" like a big chocolate cake, but I was escorted from the post office when I tried to send lit candles through the mail. Here's a card instead. You can eat it if you want, but I wouldn't. Paper's pretty hard to digest.

63. Something really important happened on this day in history: you were born. Happy Birthday!

64. I remember the day you were born like it was yesterday. Wait, you're how old? Now I feel ANCIENT! Thanks a lot, jerk! Oh yeah, and have a happy birthday or whatever.

65. I'm closing my eyes to wish you the greatest birthday EVER (that's why my writing's so messy). Happy B-Day!

66. You're all that and a bag of chips! On another note, we're out of chips. Can I eat you instead?

67. I wish you a very happy birthday. Also, I wish for a million wishes. What do you mean you're not a genie?

68. It's never too early or too late to become a crazy cat lady. Just sayin'. (P.S. You should probably start taking those calcium pills right about now.)

69. Thank you for being a friend, my fellow Golden Girl.

70. Whenever I think of you, I smile. And I think about you a lot, so I probably look like an idiot. Oh well. You're worth it. Happy Birthday!

71. Here's to a friend who gets better with age. Like fine wine. Or smelly cheese. Not that you stink… that's totally not what I meant. Anyway, have a good one.

72. Youth is a time for pursuing idealistic goals and protesting everything that's unfair in the world. Sounds exhausting! Better you than me. Happy Birthday!

73. I've searched high and low, and I haven't found another friend as great as you. I also can't find my wallet, so I guess you'll be paying for dinner. Happy Birthday! (and I'm kidding about dinner… unless you've got a heap of extra cash lying around…)

74. It's not easy being a princess, but you pull it off beautifully. Today's your day! (but, honestly, what day isn't?)

75. I considered buying you a really extravagant birthday gift this year, but then I remembered... I'm broke! So Happy Birthday. Hope you like cards.

76. Redeem this card for one free full-body massage at Big Larry's Lube, Oil and Filter. (Kidding!) Have a good one, buddy.

77. Only a few more years until you can snag that senior's discount. The countdown begins...

78. If laughter is the best medicine, whip out that prescription and we'll celebrate your birthday full-out. Happy Birthday!

79. Did I ever tell you how lucky I feel to have a friend like you? There's nothing like an old crow to make me feel like a spring chicken. Have a good one!

80. You know you're getting older when constipation is your favourite topic of

conversation. Have a happy birthday, and may your bowels run wild and free!

81. I'm not saying you're old, but it might be a good idea to keep a fire extinguisher handy when you light your handles. Have a brilliant birthday!

LOVEY-DOVEY

82. You make every other day of the year about me. Today is all about you. You want it? You got it! Happy Birthday!

83. I'll tell you I love you 365 times: one "I love you" for every day of the year. On your next birthday, I'll do it again. I'll do it every year, because I'll love you forever!

84. There is nothing in this world more special to me than you. I hope you have a wonderful birthday. You deserve it.

85. Nobody else has touched my heart in quite the way you have. I'm so thankful to have you in my life. Happy Birthday!

86. For everything we are, everything we have been, and everything we will be, I wish you a very happy birthday.

87. I tried to count every little thing I love about you, but the list goes on forever. I love you for everything that makes up the very special YOU in my life. Happy Birthday!

88. We may not always see eye to eye, but for your birthday I want to set all the petty squabbles aside and celebrate everything I love about you. We're stronger than anything that could possibly come between us.

89. Every day I wake up next to you, my life looks a little brighter. Thank you for being there every morning, noon, and night. I love you. Happy Birthday!

90. With every year we're together, you grow more special to me. Thanks for your unwavering support. I appreciate you more than you'll ever know. Happy Birthday!

91. Lots of love on your special day. I'm honoured you're spending it with me.

92. Wherever I go and whatever I do, I hold your heart in my heart and your smile in my mind. You're the greatest thing that's ever happened to me. Have a wonderful birthday!

93. You're special to me every day of the year, but my brightest and most loving thoughts are reserved especially for your birthday.

94. Life has brought me endless joy since we first met. Thank you for sharing your special day, and all your days, with me.

95. When I wish you a happy birthday, I'm not just saying I hope you have a good day. I'm saying I'm glad to have you in my life. The planet just wouldn't be the same without you.

96. Your birthday is the perfect time to tell you how important you are to me. How many times have you listened to my silly complaints and supported me through challenging moments? I don't know what I would do without you. Thank you for always being there at my side.

97. I know it's your birthday, but I have one very special request: please, don't ever stop being the amazing, incredible, loving, trustworthy, wonderful person you've been since the moment we met. I adore you exactly as you are. Happy Birthday!

98. Like flowers in the garden of life, our love blossoms more beautifully and fragrantly with

every passing year. Here's to you and your birthday as we celebrate another year together.

99. I may not always know what to say, but still waters run deep. I want you to know I feel my love for you right down to the depths of my soul. I hope you have the happiest birthday of your life!

100. Every time you look at this card, I hope you'll remember how much I truly care about you— not just today, but every day. Have a very happy birthday and never forget how much I love you!

101. It's never enough to just say Happy Birthday to the most important person in your life. The trouble is, I don't know how to express how much I love and appreciate having you in my world. The words don't exist. So I guess I'll just say "Happy Birthday" after all, and spend the rest of the year showing you exactly how much you mean to me.

What Should I Write?

101 Wishes of Congratulations for Greeting Cards

Madeleine Mayfair

Do you freeze up every time a greeting card gets passed your way? Everybody else seems to know exactly what to write. Why does your mind goes blank? What do you do?

Consult this book!

It contains 101 unique sentiments you can write in

congratulatory cards for friends, family, or co-workers. Is someone in your life having a baby? Getting married? Buying a new house? Graduating from high school, college or university? If an anniversary is coming up or someone you know got a new job or a divorce (yes, you read that right) then it's time to grab a copy of this ebook!

Kick your fear of "Blank Inside" cards to the curb. Or put your artistic skills to use and make your own! No need to worry about what you'll write inside.

You can conquer any congratulatory card with "What Should I Write? 101 Wishes of Congratulations for Greeting Cards."

NEW HOME

1. Congratulations on your new house. May your move mark the beginning of a life filled with peace, joy and everything you hold dear.

2. I can't believe you bought your first house before I did. Pardon me as I stifle my jealousy. (Kidding!)

3. A home is so much more than a floor, some walls and a roof. A home is a place filled with

comfort and love. It's the place you go to in your mind when life gets stressful. May your new house become a home to you in no time.

4. Best wishes as you fill your new home with the building blocks of treasured memories.

5. This little greeting comes your way to extend congratulations on a BIG life event. Congrats on the new house!

6. May your new home provide the ideal setting for happiness today, tomorrow and always.

7. Heard you bought a new place. When's the housewarming party? You put out the chips and I'll bring the booze!

8. Just a small gift for your new place. I hope every time you look at it your house will feel a little more like home.

9. Hats off to the new house! And shoes off, too. No feet on the coffee table. Boy oh boy, you just moved in and already you're bossing us around. Just kidding! I'm really happy for you.

BABY

10. There's nothing more beautiful in life than a happy parent beaming over a newborn child. Please let me extend my most heartfelt congratulations on the new addition to your family.

11. May the day you meet your child be the first in a lifetime of happiness. Here's to an ideal adoption and a joyful life ahead for you and your new family!

12. I hope your baby grows up to be just like you: caring, generous, and wonderful to be around!

13. Best wishes for baby. Best wishes for you. Heartfelt congratulations on your bundle of joy!

14. Your child is truly a gift. May you always cherish the most special bond two people can share.

15. A hopeful wish for a life of bliss as you greet your child for the first time. Congratulations on your day of adoption!

16. May all your days of rearing your wonderful child bring you more fulfillment than you could ever imagine. Heartfelt congratulations!

17. Celebrating with you as you bring new life into the world. May your love live on forever in the spirit of your precious child!

18. Congratulations on the birth of your child. May you always recall the blissful moment when you first held your baby in your arms.

19. In your heart there will always be a cuddly warm place with your child's name on it. I want you to know there's a place in my heart for both of you, and it will be there forever.

20. Who ever imagined such a tiny being could create such huge love in the hearts of everyone around? Felicitations on the new arrival!

21. With special thoughts on the occasion of your baby's birth. May the first days of your new child's life bring you the greatest bliss imaginable.

22. Your life is about to change forever. Here's hoping your days are more cuddly bunnies than stepping on Legos!

23. Wishing you the happiest days of your life as you usher your first child into the world. Heartfelt congratulations!

24. May this new child fill your world with peace, tranquility and plenty of full nights' sleep. If that doesn't happen (and it probably won't!) at least your life will be a wild adventure from here on in!

25. With my best good wishes for you and baby, I offer my heartfelt congratulations.

WEDDING

26. Here's to a life that's filled with laughter, love and devotion. Congratulations on your marriage!

27. Wishing you a beautiful wedding day and long, loving years of happy marriage ahead!

28. Along with every other joy your wedding day will bring, I wish you some small moment that's so full of quiet pleasure that it stays fresh in your mind forever. Congratulations on the ideal marriage!

29. I'm so glad you two got together. You're a match made in heaven!

30. From this day forward you'll know what it means to share everything: happiness and heartache, laughter and tears. Life isn't always smooth sailing, but you'll have each other to cling to while you ride out the storms, and you'll have each other's embrace to bask in on those lovely sunny days. My wish for you is

simply that life hands you more sun than storms. Congratulations on your marriage.

31. A wedding wish for two great people who mean so much to each other. Heartfelt congratulations on your special day!

32. I hope all your dreams come true as you settle into a life of endless laughter. Congratulations!

33. Two great people like you deserve a wedding day that pulls out all the stops. Here's to you and your wedding too!

34. Congratulations! May each and every year of married life grow in sweetness and in joy.

35. You deserve the best. Thank goodness you found each other! Congratulations on your marriage!

36. Who wishes you all the best? Who hopes you'll be happy for years to come? Who always thought you two were perfect for each other? Why, that would be me! Congratulations!

37. May your wedding day mark the beginning of a marriage full of warmth, love, and endless adoration. Congratulations to you both!

38. A wedding wish for two wonderful people as you embark on one happy life together. Congratulations!

39. Once in a lifetime, that special person comes along and your heart cries out: This is right! I'm so happy you listened to your hearts. May your wedding day be as much fun as everything leading up to it!

40. A match made in heaven? Yeah, that's you. Happy Wedding Day!

41. Hope this small gift will help you establish a happy home. Warm hugs and best wishes as you start a new life together!

42. Congratulations on your wedding. Wishing you joy every day hereafter.

43. Best wishes for a beautiful wedding day and an eternally happy life together!

44. I hope every moment of this fine wedding day reminds you how special you are to all your family and friends, and how much we want to celebrate your happiness. Congratulations!

ANNIVERSARY

45. It's my pleasure to wish you a happy anniversary as you celebrate a love that was meant to be. Congratulations and Best Wishes!

46. Seems like only yesterday you stood in front of all your family and friends, said your vows, and dedicated your hearts to one another. In the years that have passed, it's been a joy to watch your love grow. Here's to a happy anniversary and many delightful days to come!

47. May this year's anniversary fill your hearts with the kind of happiness only the most precious partnership can bring!

48. You both said, "YES!" and then everybody cheered and then we drank a whole lot… and things are a little hazy after that. In fact, I'm amazed I remember your wedding at all. But I could never forget your anniversary! Have a good one!

49. All these years and still going strong! Here's to you and your marvellous marriage. Happy Anniversary!

50. Happy Anniversary to the couple that never makes me feel like a third wheel when I tag along because I don't have a date. Also... do you know anyone who might be interested? Nah, never mind. Today's all about you. But think about it and let me know tomorrow.

51. You were right for each other from the very beginning. It's no surprise a couple as perfect as you has made it this far. Happy Anniversary!

52. Your wedding anniversary is a special day to reflect on the wonderful times you've shared. Today, celebrate the love that is yours and yours alone.

53. May the years ahead bring even more love, good times, laughter and bliss than you've ever known. Happiness always and heartfelt congratulations!

54. On this very special anniversary, we wish you a joyous celebration of the years you've spent

together and the life that's yet to come. Congratulations!

55. The tides of life never cease to change, but no matter how harshly the winds have howled your love has never altered its course. Here's to a couple that can temper any storm. Happy Anniversary!

56. Wishing you a wonderful anniversary and many happy years to come!

57. You've shared so many happy days. You've worked to build a life together. Now reap the reward of peace that you so very much deserve. Happy Anniversary!

58. No matter how you spend your day, here's hoping every minute is full of bliss!

59. Happy Anniversary to a couple that shares more love and laughter than anyone else I know. You two are great together!

60. Your love has inspired so many of us to strive for the loving relationship you've achieved. Wishing you a spectacular anniversary!

GRADUATION

61. Graduation day is a source of pride not only for you, but for everyone in your life. We're all so pleased you've made it this far!

62. You've worked so hard to arrive at this day. Take pride in everything you've accomplished. Happy Graduation!

63. May your graduation day fill your heart with as much pride as I'm feeling for you right now. You've done so well. Congratulations!

64. A simple card can't begin to express how proud we are, or how often we've thought of you while you were away at school. We hope you always knew you had us in your corner.

65. It's your day to celebrate, Grad! Wishing you every success as you enter the working world.

66. May this small token of our esteem show you how proud we are that you've successfully completed your schooling. Congratulations on your graduation!

67. When I think of how much you've accomplished in just a few short years, it makes me incredibly proud. You can do anything you put your mind to. Enjoy Graduation Day!

68. Wishing you pride on your graduation day and years of fulfilling work ahead!

69. Celebrate your success! You deserve it. I know how hard you worked to get here.

70. The friendships you've formed in your school days will stay with you forever if you cultivate and cherish them. May your happiness build as you move into the great big world.

71. May your goals and aspirations remain as high tomorrow as they are today. Congratulations on your graduation.

72. You've got a bright future ahead of you, whether you realize it or not. Nobody knows what life has in store and you may go through lots of different jobs before you find the one that suits you best, but don't let that worry you. You don't need to know everything right this second. Once you find your groove I know you'll go far.

73. Congratulations, New Grad! I told 'ya you could do it… and I was right!

74. Time to celebrate everything you've accomplished. Your future holds such promise and I know you'll succeed beyond your wildest dreams. Congratulations, Grad!

75. Graduation day is the perfect time to celebrate the knowledge you've acquired, the path you've chosen, and the fun you've had in the process. Congratulations!

76. Your hard work and perseverance have been an inspiration. I hope you're as proud of your achievement as I am of you. Congratulations!

NEW JOB

77. My sincerest congratulations as you embark on this new endeavour!

78. May your new job bring you all kinds of sappy feel-good emotions. May it also earn you bags and bags of cold hard cash!

79. What's the point of trudging every day to a job you can't stand? So many people do it and it's such a waste. I'm glad you've set off on a career path you can really sink your teeth into. A toast to doing what you love!

80. Hooray! Woo-hoo! Here's to you and your new job too!

81. Now that you've snagged your new job maybe you could pick up the tab once in a while when we go out for drinks. Naaaaaah, just kidding. (I'm not kidding.) Anyway, good going on the new job.

82. You were a real hit around the office from the first day you started here. I know you're going to make a splash at the new place too!

83. Congrats on the promotion. I knew you could do it!

84. Now that you've found a brand new path, here's hoping it leads to wild success. Congratulations on your new job!

85. May this new job fill your life with purpose and satisfaction. Congratulations!

86. The first day at a new job can be a nerve-wracking experience, but when you've got what it takes to achieve great things there's no need to be anxious. Get out there and show 'em what you've got!

87. As you strive for success, don't ever forget to share your many talents with the world. Let your light shine and your happiness will build.

88. You've got the skills. You've got the know-how. What's next? Putting them to good use! Congrats on the new job. I know you'll be just great.

89. Hate to be a buzz-kill, but you'll never have as much fun at any other workplace, and you'll never find a group of co-workers who laugh at

your jokes as hard as we do. But you're moving on. As much as we'll all miss you, we're happy for you too. Congrats on the new job!

90. Wishing you happiness on your first day of work and every other day to follow!

91. Good going on the promotion. Told 'ya you were the best candidate!

92. We wish you the best. Don't be a stranger!

93. Wherever you go and whatever you do, you can bet we'll all be missing you. Good luck with the new job!

DIVORCE

94. It may sound strange to congratulate someone on the end of a relationship, but you've been through some tough times over the last little while and I'm glad you've regained your freedom. Here's to a life of liberty!

95. You've always been there for me, through thick and thin. I just want you to know I'm with you, whether you want to cry on my shoulder or party all night long!

96. I don't want to say anything negative about your marriage, but if it wasn't right for you I'm glad you decided to step away. Let me know when you want to get out there and I'll put on my dancing shoes!

97. Sending encouragement and happy thoughts as you start the next phase of your life. Imagine the possibilities!

98. Now that you're moving on, accept my warmest wishes for happiness in the future.

99. Here's wishing you a time in life where freedom reins and happiness is your sky.

100. Life holds so many choices and sometimes it's hard to know whether we're making the right ones. Only you can know for sure, and if you feel in your heart that you're striking off on the proper path, I'll be there to support and encourage you.

101. Wishing you all the fun and excitement that only the second phase of life can bring!

101 Father's Day Wishes for Greeting Cards

What Should I Write?

Madeleine Mayfair

Sometimes it's hard to find the right words, especially when you're writing out a Father's Day card. You want to express yourself in a way that's heartfelt without being too sappy. Or maybe you just want to make your cool dad laugh. Either way, you can put a smile on his face with words that reflect the kind of relationship you share. In this collection, you'll find sentiments applicable to biological fathers, adoptive dads, stepdads, fathers-in-law, grandfathers or any man who plays a fatherly role in your life

Kick your fear of "Blank Inside" cards to the curb. Or put your artistic skills to use and make your own! No need to worry about what you'll write inside.

Whether your relationship is difficult or idyllic, you're sure to find the ideal sentiment for Dad in "What Should I Write? 101 Father's Day Wishes for Greeting Cards."

SHORT AND SWEET

1. Happy Father's Day to the best dad in the world!

2. This is a day to celebrate YOU. Get out there and have some fun. Happy Father's Day!

3. You're an amazing dad! Just thought I'd remind you, in case you'd forgotten. Happy Father's Day!

4. Happy Father's Day to a dad who's also a good buddy.

5. I don't know how the rest of the world feels about their dads, but I know I'd be lost without you.

6. I hope this Father's Day reminds you how important you are to everyone in your life, and especially to me.

7. Most people think love is a four letter word, but to me it only has three: D-A-D

8. I don't know what my life would be like today if I'd never learned all the things you took such care to teach me.

9. You're the greatest dad any kid could hope for. Happy Father's Day!

10. I can't thank you enough for all the wonderful things you've done over the years. Thank you! Thank you! Thank you!

11. I love my dad THIS MUCH! Happy Father's Day!

12. Every time I need you, you're always there. Thanks for being the kind of dad I can count on.

13. For all your thoughtfulness, I send this card with my fondest appreciation. Happy Father's Day!

14. Hope you have a really fun Father's Day! Sorry I can't be there, but you'll be in my thoughts all day long.

15. Father's Day will always be a special event in our family because you are so special to all of us. Enjoy your day!

16. I hope this Father's Day is just like you: full of love and fun and sunny brightness!

17. For me, Father's Day is every day... because you are always there for me. I love you, Dad!

18. Thanks for every little thoughtful thing you do. I'm so lucky to have a dad like you!

19. May this Father's Day fill your spirit with the summer fun!

20. No matter what each day brings, I smile because you're in it. Happy Father's Day!

21. This Father's Day, I wish you every joy in the world!

HEARTFELT

22. You've never been shy about telling the world you're proud to be my dad. I want you to know I'm every bit as proud to call myself your child. Happy Father's Day!

23. Sometimes we have disagreements. You want one thing, and I want something totally different. I know I often resist what's best for me, but it's reassuring to know there's someone in the world who always has my best interests at heart. Happy Father's Day.

24. I love you for all the times I needed you and you were there. I love you for all the times I needed space and you let me achieve my goals on my own. Thanks for supporting me and thank you for letting me fly.

25. Some people are lucky in life. They've got health and wealth and laughter and love. But you know why I'm lucky? Because I've got you as a father. You're the best. Happy Father's Day!

26. If there's one thing I can count on, it's that every time I pick up the phone, you'll be there at the other end. Thanks for always listening when I need to talk. Happy Father's Day!

27. I know we haven't been on the best of terms lately, but that doesn't mean I love you any less. I'll always be your kid and you'll always be my dad. Happy Father's Day.

28. Remember when I was a teenager and I disobeyed you at every turn? Did you ever think, back then, that we'd end up being so close? I sure didn't, but I'm so thankful life worked out this way. Happy Father's Day!

29. For all the times I never say it and all the times you so deserved it, I love you, Dad. What would I do without you in my life?

30. It's no coincidence that Father's Day falls at a time of year when the summer sun shines so hard. Those bright skies never fail to remind me of that smile you beam when you're especially proud. I hope you have a truly wonderful day!

31. If everyone had a Father like you, the world would be a much better place. Happy Father's Day!

32. May this Father's Day create memories that will live in your heart forever.

33. Back when I was a kid, it always made me so mad when I was taking something super-seriously and you were just standing there laughing. Now that I'm older, I understand that you laughed when you were uncomfortable or didn't know how to react. So go ahead and laugh at this heartfelt card, if you want to. Today is your day.

34. When I was younger, I thought my dad was a superhero. It's hard to believe any human could accomplish everything you've done in life. To be honest, you're still my superhero.

35. I can only hope to be half the person you are. Thank you for always being there. Happy Father's Day!

36. Do you know how much I appreciate everything you give me throughout the year? Well, today

it's my turn to give back. Don't be afraid to put me to work. Housework? Yard work? Shine your shoes? Polish your car? Whatever you want done, I'll get right on it. Happy Father's Day!

37. Here's wishing you a day that brings not only rest and relaxation, but joy, laughter and togetherness. This day is all yours!

38. Seems like you've got a busier life in retirement than you had when you were working. How did that happen, exactly? Well, take a load off. Today is YOUR day.

39. With every year that passes, you become an even more important part of my life. Nobody could ever replace you, Dad.

40. Being the only parent in the house made it extra hard on you, but that never stopped you from rising to the occasion and being the best parent a person could have. Happy Father's Day.

41. You've never been the easiest person to please, but every time you smile because I've done

something right, I feel great about my accomplishments. Happy Father's Day!

42. Sometimes you say I'm too serious, but you know what? Over the years, you've taught me to laugh a little more.

43. Dad, you've been such a great teacher and an unbelievable support. Happy Father's Day!

44. Commercials and cards characterize fathers as those guys who fish and watch TV and BBQ burgers, but you're so much more and you know it. Happy Father's Day to a dad who'll never be a cardboard cut-out.

45. No matter where I go and what I do, I know you're always thinking of me and hoping for the best. Dad, I only wish you knew how much your support means … because it means a whole lot.

46. Now that I'm a parent too, I know how hard it is to maintain a positive outlook all the time. How on earth did you do that, Dad? You always made us feel like everything was going to work out.

47. Happy Father's Day to a dad who does the impossible all the time.

48. Whenever I'm feeling down, I only have to think of you. You've always got the answers to any of life's little problems. Happy Father's Day!

49. I've got so little to give to someone who has given me so much. Big Hug! Big Kiss! Lots of Love!

50. Dads make every day happy for everyone else, but my Father's Day wish is a happy day that's all yours. You deserve it!

51. You're the person who taught me to understand other people's point of view instead of mindlessly arguing or thinking I was right all the time. That's what a great father gives the world.

52. Fathers are all special people, but you stand high above the crowd. Thanks for being the kind of dad I could always look up to.

53. A Father's gift is the curiosity and inventiveness he plants in his children's imaginations. Without

a dad like you, I'd have never grown up to be a me like ME!

54. If I had to trade places with you for a day, I don't know how I would keep up! Thanks for working so relentlessly in everything you do. Happy Father's Day!

55. I don't say it enough, but I love you. Thanks for all everything you so unselfishly do. You deserve more than just one day's celebration.

56. On this day devoted to you, I hope all the kindness you've shown the world comes back tenfold. Happy Father's Day!

57. I have a great life, and I owe it all to you. You built my foundation and put a roof over my head so I'd always feel both rooted and safe. Happy Father's Day!

58. I really don't know what I would do without, Dad. You've made even the most challenging moments of my life a little easier. Thank you and Happy Father's Day!

59. You taught me to be a good parent by setting a wonderful example when I was young. Thank

you for the many gifts you've given me over the years.

60. Even though we can't see each other as often as we'd like, I want to wish you a really great Father's Day.

61. May your heart be filled with every joy you've brought me throughout my life. Happy Father's Day!

62. There are no words to describe a Father like you. I don't know how so much love, compassion, sacrifice, warmth, joy, energy and life could be wrapped up in one person. But there you are. Happy Father's Day!

63. There's no such thing as a perfect parent. I know you sometimes wonder if you should have done things differently or been a "better dad," but I want you to know you did just fine raising me. Holding grudges would only hurt the relationship we're establishing now. I really am glad to have you in my life, Dad.

64. The relationship a father shares with his child can put a young person on a trail to triumph or a

path to disaster. I guess I'm one of the lucky ones. Heartfelt thanks and Happy Father's Day!

65. We haven't been able to see each other much lately, but I think we both know that it's circumstances beyond our control keeping us apart. If I had one wish, it would be to spend Father's Day together. I love you and I miss you, Dad.

66. It wasn't until I became a parent that I realized how many sacrifices you made for me when I was young. Sorry if I didn't appreciate it at the time, but I want you to know I get it now. Thank you!

SPECIFIC TO STEPDADS AND OTHER FAMILY ARRANGEMENTS

67. You haven't been my dad forever, but I've never seen my mom smile so much as she does when she glances in your direction. I look forward to getting to know you better in the years ahead.

68. It seems like only yesterday that I was acting like a total brat and saying you could never replace my "real dad." Since then, you've shown me that a real dad is one who shows he cares on a daily basis… in word, thought and action. It's sure been a rocky road, but I want to thank you for being a real dad to me.

69. To a grandfather who's always been like a dad to me: I truly appreciate all the time and effort you've devoted to raising me right. Thank you and Happy Father's Day!

70. A friend and mentor is a rare treasure. Thank you for filling my life with purpose and direction.

71. When I married into your family I knew I was getting something special, but I never could have prepared myself for how welcome I'd feel. (I was actually kind of scared of you, in the beginning!) Thanks for making your house feel like home. Happy Father's Day to a truly amazing father-in-law!

72. Thank you for bringing the joys of family to me. I feel very privileged to have you in my life. No one else will ever compare!

73. I know what it's like to be a parent, but I will never live up to the standard of perfection you set. You are the best!

74. When I think FATHER, I think YOU. Thanks for always being there.

75. Happy Father's Day, from the bottom of my heart, to the guy who was always there for me even when nobody else was.

76. I haven't always been the perfect child, but you've always been an outstanding parent. Thanks for being strong when I was weak.

77. What could be better than one great dad? Two great dads, of course! Thanks for all the love and support you both show me throughout the year. Happy Father's Day!

78. Every so often, a special person walks into your life. After that, you wonder how you ever lived without them. Thank you for being the father figure I've always needed.

79. Dad, no matter where we are on the planet, whether we are liberated or captive, in our hearts we will always be free. Happy Father's Day to you.

80. I used to get upset when you said no, but now I see it was all about making me a stronger person. Thank you for being the resolute, determined individual you are. I am better for your discipline.

81. Happy Father's Day from someone who loves you as unconditionally as you've always loved me.

82. A lot of people complain about their in-laws, but not me. Not ever. I'm one of the lucky ones.

I've got a father-in-law who treats me like I'm one of his own crazy kids. Happy Father's Day!

83. Happy Father's Day to a grandpa who's about so much more than fishin' and whittlin'!

84. Of all the special people in my life, there could never be anyone more special than you. Thanks for teaching me to trust again. Happy Father's Day!

FUNNY AND FUN

85. Remember when I was a kid? Yeah, me neither. That was a million years ago. Man, are we getting old. Anyway, Happy Father's Day!

86. I don't want to get all sappy on you, Dad. That's just not who we are. Instead, I'll thank you for everything you do while I madly raid the refrigerator. You weren't going to eat this potato salad, were you?

87. Some people don't understand why I still live at home, but if they had a dad as cool as you, they'd all live at home too. I will always be your loving and eternally grateful freeloader!

88. What you lack in cooking and cleaning skills, you more than make up for in awesomeness!

89. Sending you my love through the mail. Hope it gets there in one piece (and on time). Happy Father's Day!

90. Father's Day is the perfect opportunity to treat yourself to something delicious. Have a burger. Have some cake. Have a little more. And some

ice cream, too! And maybe another burger!
(It's your day. Enjoy it!)

91. My friend + my sidekick + the best dressed guy
on the block = my dad. Happy Father's Day!

92. I don't want to get cheesy about it, but I
appreciate all the funny faces you make, all the
jokes you crack and all the love you give.
You're the best. Happy Father's Day!

93. Happy Happy Happy Happy Happy Happy
Happy Father's Day. Now aren't you glad I
never totally lost that stutter?

94. They say I've got a face only a mother could
love. Well, you seem pretty okay with it, too.
Thanks for being there, Dad!

95. I know I was a little hell-raiser when I was
younger. Oh, who am I kidding? I'm still a hell-
raiser now! Thanks for putting up with me.
Happy Father's Day!

96. The term "World's Greatest Dad" gets brandied
about a lot these days, but everybody around
here knows the title is yours. Have a good one—
you deserve it!

97. I didn't bring a gift, but I did bring my laundry. Get on that, will ya? Happy Father's Day!

98. Growing up, all my friends were so jealous of me because I had the fun dad. What they didn't know is that I was always jealous of YOU. You were way more fun than I was.

99. You are the most important person in the world to me… and not just because you're letting me live in your house rent-free! (You're also a pretty great dad. And a wizard with my taxes!)

100. Is there anything you could do to make yourself a better dad? Nah, of course not! Well… maybe get a tattoo. That would be pretty cool. Happy Father's Day!

101. Happy Father's Day!!! For me, it's a 365 day celebration… except for leap years, when it's 366 days. I love you, Dad!

Do you freeze up every time a greeting card gets passed around the office? Everybody else seems to know exactly what to write. Why does your mind go blank? What do you do?

Consult this book!

It contains 101 unique sentiments you can write in get well cards for friends, family members, or co-workers. You'll find everything from tender reassurances and heartfelt well-wishes to cheerful rhymes, as well as realistic expressions of hope, care and concern. If someone in your life is injured, under the weather or battling illness and you just can't seem to find the right words, then it's time to grab a copy of this ebook!

Kick your fear of "Blank Inside" cards to the curb. Or put your artistic skills to use and make your own! No need to worry about what you'll write inside.

You can conquer any get well card with "What Should I Write? 101 Get Well Wishes for Greeting Cards."

SHORT AND SWEET

1. So sorry to hear you've been unwell. Hope you're on the mend!

2. I hope this card puts a smile on your face by reminding you someone truly cares. Get well soon!

3. We've missed you around the office. Hope you feel better soon!

4. Even when there's nobody around, I want you to know you are never alone. Let our well-

wishes warm your heart and hasten your recovery.

5. At this difficult time, I'm sending warm thoughts and wishes for good health your way.

6. Just a little note to say I hope you're feeling better today. Get well soon!

7. Sending love, good wishes and encouragement when you're feeling unwell.

8. Here's wishing you a return to good health. May each day feel a little brighter than the last!

9. You're the kind of person who always puts a smile on everyone else's face. Hope this card puts a smile on yours. Get well soon!

10. Wishing you rest, relaxation and rejuvenation.

11. Gentle thoughts for good health to come.

12. Take care of yourself. You'll be feeling healthy and strong again in no time.

13. When you're away from the office it's like rainclouds descend on the place. Hope you feel better soon so you can bring back the sun!

14. Life is what you make of it, and you've made mine beautiful. I hope you feel better soon.

15. While you're in hospital, we want you to know that everything is well and good around here. Don't worry about work! You just concentrate on getting better.

16. Wishing you sunny days ahead. Thinking of you and hoping you'll soon feel well again.

17. Sending special wishes that health will return very soon.

18. So happy to hear that you're starting to feel better!

19. Encouraging thoughts are with you as your health improves.

20. Here's hoping good health soon returns to one of the most special people I know.

21. Hope you'll be up and about and feeling a whole lot better very, very soon!

22. May yesterday's adventures bolster your spirits as you fight to regain good health.

23. Heard you were sick. Well, that's no good! Is there anything I can do to help while you're out of commission?

24. I have tremendous faith that every day you'll feel a little better in some small way.

25. With love and compassion as you recover.

26. The memories of fun times we've shared help to keep you close while you're away. Hope you feel better soon. We miss you!

27. Hope you're feeling right as rain before long. Get well soon!

28. The gift of good health is on its way. I can see it from here! You'll feel better very soon.

29. Here's hoping, in a very short while, you'll be out of that bed for good!

30. Looking forward to toasting your recovery!

31. Warm thoughts are coming at you each and every day. Hope you feel better very soon!

32. Just a sunny little reminder that someone out there is thinking of you. Get well soon!

33. Warm wishes for a quick recovery. Call me any time you need a friend.

34. Sending healing energy your way as you recover.

35. A note of cheer from all of us who are thinking of you. We wish you were here! Get well soon!

36. In the time you've been off work nobody's been able to fill your shoes. We think about you every day and hope for a speedy recovery.

37. Just a simple little message full of warm wishes. Here's to a quick recovery!

38. Here's hoping you'll feel good as new in no time.

39. Nothing can take you down, buddy. You'll be up and at 'em in no time. Just you wait and see.

40. May good health find its way back home and strengthen you, body and soul.

41. We're hoping our collective will can sway the tides and bring you the best of health. Get well soon!

42. I want you to know I'm here for you. Tell me what you need and consider it done.

HEARTFELT

43. A simple card can't begin to express how often we think of you or how warmly we hold you in our hearts. Get well soon!

44. Thinking of you at this time when wellness seems a long way off. It's not out of reach. Trust me. You'll get there.

45. I won't sugar-coat my message of hope. I know you're going through a terrible time right now. I know you don't want to hear useless platitudes. But I also know you're one of the strongest people I've ever met. If anyone can beat this thing, it's you.

46. The measure of a true friendship is not how it flutters across life's sunny days, but how it weathers out the storms. I want to be a true friend to you, now and forever. You can always count on me.

47. Things may seem dark right now, but this long night will pass. When the morning sun shines on you, it will shine with a brightness that mends your body and soothes your soul.

48. It's hard to know what to say at a time like this. "Get well" seems rather trite. You deserve so

much more. But until I can think up the perfect wish I'll just tell you you're in my thoughts. Health will be yours again soon.

49. Friends as fine as you don't come along every day. That's why I want to wish you good health and recovery. I need you by my side!

50. Here's wishing you a day free of pain, when the whole word is sunny and the skies of the future shine bright.

51. Please know that you're in our thoughts. You have our warmest understanding and most ardent friendship as you heal.

52. May your faith bring you comfort and soften your pain. Strength is yours and health is on the way.

53. If you'd rather go it alone, I'll be cheering you on from here. If you'd rather walk with the strength of a friend, I'll be right there at your side. I wish you a quick recovery, whichever path you choose.

54. Nobody deserves to get sick, and you never think it'll happen to someone you care about so deeply. That's why, when it does, nobody really knows what to say. I'm sorry if I don't have the

right words when you need them, but I want you to know how much I care. I'm here for you.

55. Take a rest. You push yourself too hard. It's time to sit back and let others care for you until you're well again. Relax for a while. You deserve it.

56. May the knowledge that so many people are on your side bring you solace and strength to battle this illness.

57. Every day, I close my eyes and make a little wish. If wishes do come true, you'll feel healthy and strong in no time. Meanwhile, please know you're always in my thoughts.

58. It's my sincerest hope that you're on your way to a speedy recovery. I wish you the best of health.

59. Maybe cheerful good wishes aren't what you want to hear right now. Maybe you just want someone to sit beside you and show you, in actions rather than words, that they care deeply for your wellbeing. I can be that person. Whatever you need.

60. Just a little note to say I'm keeping you in my thoughts and hoping you'll feel better before long.

61. May the joy you've brought everyone in your life return to you tenfold. Warm wishes for a speedy recovery.

62. At this time when you're not feeling your best, may you draw strength from the affection of your friends. You have my unfaltering support.

63. They say friends make everything better. Too bad our friendship can't miraculously cure you! I would do anything to see you up and about like usual.

64. You've always filled my days with sunshine, and now it's my turn. Let me know what I can do to make life sparkle. I'm here for you.

65. I know I can't magically make you better, but if there are any practical day-to-day things you'd like me to do, I'd be more than happy to lend a hand. I want to help you in any way I can.

66. During this time of illness, may the beauty of life shine on you like the sun breaking through clouds on a rainy day. All will be well soon.

67. Sometimes all we have to hold on to is faith that things will get better. I trust, with all my heart, that you will be well again. Until then, let me know if there's anything I can do.

68. You're sick and that sucks. There's no sugar-coating it. Sometimes the thought makes me angry or sad or just leaves me feeling totally helpless—and I'm not even the one who's sick! I really can't imagine what you're going through right now, but I want you to know I'm thinking of you.

69. I hope this card serves as a reminder that you're very special to many, many people. Wishing you a speedy recovery and brighter days ahead.

CUTE AND CHEERFUL

70. This card contains millions of microscopic get-well wishes. Hope they'll help you feel better as soon as possible!

71. Warm and cheery wishes from a friend who hopes to see you fully recovered and feeling fine soon!

72. May this little note plant a seed of hope in your heart that grows into strength and recovery.

73. Please know that I will always care. Please know that I am always there. Get well soon!

74. The world's warmest greetings are coming your way with hopes you'll feel better without delay. Get well soon!

75. Cheery wishes and friendly smiles can light the path for miles and miles. Hope you're feeling better!

76. They say you'll break if you don't bend, so I want you to know I'll be your friend through all the days you're on the mend!

77. Hello, you! Is there anything I can do? Getting sick surely wasn't your plan, but I'll help in any way I can. Hope you feel better soon!

78. More thoughts than ever are coming your way. Here's hoping you feel better each and every day.

79. I think of you often, and I hope you know I do, but there's something about an illness that makes it especially true. Get well soon!

80. We miss you while you're out sick, sick, sick! Hope you start feeling better quick, quick, quick!

81. Friendly thoughts are coming your way with hopes that they will brighten your day!

82. I heard you're not feeling great, but I know you. Before long, you'll be feeling good as new!

83. Picture me sending a fragrant bouquet of sunny warm wishes straight your way. Get well soon… and hopefully today!

84. What words can I possibly say to send a quick recovery your way? Only that I hope you're on the mend, and I'm always happy to be your friend!

85. We're hoping that you'll find some way to feel much better, day to day. Get well soon!

86. Nobody could ever tell that you've been feeling so unwell. Your smile could chase the clouds

away, and send them off without delay. Lookin' good, as always!

87. I get a kick out of friends like you, so let's give this illness the boot!

88. We share a smile to show we care, to show that we are always there. That's why I shine my smile at you every time you say A-CHOO!

FUN AND FUNNY

89. If a singing telegram could cure your illness, I'd sent one to your door at seven every morning. But that would probably get on your nerves, so I opted for this card instead. Get well soon or I'm sending a barbershop quartet!

90. Needing help doesn't make you weak—it means you're human. You've helped me in a million ways. It's payback time!

91. There's plenty to bitch and moan about when you're feeling crappy. Bitch and moan in my direction, please. I love that sort of stuff!

92. They say wine and cheese improve with age, so here's a get-well wish for my whiniest, cheesiest friend! (Just kidding!) But seriously, I hope you feel better soon.

93. Warmest wishes are yours to keep. Now take a bath and get some sleep! (You know you need it—the sleep, not the bath. I'm not saying you stink. That wouldn't be very nice, would it? Now, if I can just get my foot out of my mouth I'll tell you to GET WELL SOON!)

94. If I were an adorable little puppy dog, I'd lick your face until you felt all better. But I'm

human so I'll just offer my sincerest get well wishes without licking you at all. Unless you really want me to. No, that would be weird.

95. I know you inside-out, and you know I'm always right. That's why you should believe me when I say you'll be up and at 'em in no time.

96. Feeling better? No? How about now? Not yet? How about NOW? Wow, this is taking forever. I'm going to get a sandwich. (Just joking! You know I'm in your corner for the long haul.)

97. So you caught a bug, did you? You silly person! What were you chasing bugs for in the first place? (Kidding. Hope you get well soon.)

98. Candies and chocolates and cupcakes and pie. No, I'm not just naming the foods you can't eat—I'm trying to tell you there's no greater treat than spending time with you! (Also, bacon. Just thought I'd throw that in.)

99. Magic Eightball says your recovery will be swift. And Magic Eightball's never wrong, so you'd better believe it!

100. My spidey sense tells me you'll be feeling better soon. And you know what they say about the spidey sense: only Spiderman has it.

Basically what I'm telling you is that I'm Spiderman. Also, get well soon.

101. Everyone around the office is missing your smile, your charm, your hard-working nature… not to mention your lunches. What are we supposed to steal from the fridge while you're away? (Kidding. Get well soon!)

101 Mother's Day Wishes for Greeting Cards

What Should I Write?

Madeleine Mayfair

Sometimes it's hard to find the right words, especially when you're writing out a Mother's Day card. You want to express yourself in a way that's heartfelt without being too sappy. Or maybe you just want to make your cool mom laugh. Either way, you can put a smile on her face with words that reflect the kind of relationship you share. In this collection, you'll find original sentiments applicable to biological mothers, adoptive moms, step-moms, mothers-in-law, grandmothers or any woman who plays a special role in your life

Kick your fear of "Blank Inside" cards to the curb. Or put your artistic skills to use and make your own! No need to worry about what you'll write inside.

Whether your relationship is difficult or idyllic, you're sure to find the ideal sentiment for Mom in "What Should I Write? 101 Mother's Day Wishes for Greeting Cards."

SHORT AND SWEET

1. Most people think love is a four letter word, but to me it only has three letters: M-O-M
2. You're the best mom any kid could hope for. Happy Mother's Day!
3. I can't thank you enough for all the wonderful things you've done for me over the years. Thank you! Thank you! Thank you!
4. Happy Mother's Day to a mom who's also a great friend. You really are the best!
5. I love my mom THIS MUCH! Happy Mother's Day!

6. Every time I need you, you're always there. Thanks for being the kind of mom I can always count on!

7. I hope this Mother's Day reminds you how important you are to everybody in your life, and most especially to me.

8. This is a day to celebrate YOU, so get out there and do all the things you love to do. Happy Mother's Day!

9. For all your thoughtfulness, I send this card with my fondest appreciation. Happy Mother's Day!

10. Hope you have a wonderful Mother's Day! Sorry I can't be there, but you'll be in my thoughts all day long.

11. I can't thank you enough for blessing my life with beauty. I love you, Mom!

12. Mother's Day will always be a special event in our family because you are so special to all of us. Enjoy your day!

13. You're an amazing mom! Just thought I'd remind you, in case you'd forgotten. Happy Mother's Day!

14. I hope this Mother's Day is just like you: full of love and sweetness and kindness and care.

15. Where would we be if it wasn't for our mothers? I don't know about the rest of the world, but I'd be lost without you.

16. For me, Mother's Day is every day... because you are always there for me. I love you, Mom!

17. Thanks for every little thoughtful thing you do. I'm so lucky to have a mom like you!

18. May this Mother's Day fill your heart with the joys of spring.

19. No matter what each day brings, I smile because you're in it. Happy Mother's Day!

20. This Mother's Day, I wish you every joy in the world!

HEARTFELT

21. Some people are lucky in life. They've got health and wealth and laughter and love. But you know why I'm lucky? Because I've got you as a mom. You're the best. Happy Mother's Day!

22. If there's one thing I can count on, it's that every time I pick up the phone, you'll be there on the other end. Thanks for always listening when I need to talk. Happy Mother's Day!

23. You've never been shy about telling the world you're proud to be my mom. I want you to know I'm every bit as proud to call myself your child. Happy Mother's Day!

24. Sometimes it's like you know what I need even before I do. I know I often resist what's best for me, but it's reassuring to know there's someone in the world who always has my best interests at heart. Happy Mother's Day.

25. I love you for all the times I needed you and you were there. I love you for all the times I needed

space and you let me achieve my goals on my own. Thanks for supporting me and thank you for letting me fly.

26. I know we haven't been on the best of terms lately, but that doesn't mean I love you any less. I'll always be your kid and you'll always be my mom. Happy Mother's Day.

27. Remember when I was a teenager and we were constantly ripping each other's heads off? Did you ever think, back then, that we'd end up being so close now? I sure didn't, but I'm so thankful life worked out this way. Happy Mother's Day!

28. For all the times I never say it and all the times you so deserved it, I love you, Mom. What would I do without you in my life?

29. It's no coincidence that Mother's Day falls at a time of year when the buds of May are blossoming. Those fresh blooms never fail to remind me of the love our family shares. I hope you have a truly wonderful day!

30. If everyone had a mother like you, the world would be a better place. Happy Mother's Day!

31. May this Mother's Day bring you every quiet, peaceful pleasure possible and create memories that will live in your heart forever.

32. When you laugh, you make the world such a bright place. Happy Mother's Day to the best mom in the world!

33. There are no words to express the wonders you have brought into my life. I can only hope to be half the person you are. Thank you for always being there. Happy Mother's Day!

34. Do you know how much I appreciate everything you give me throughout the year? Well, today it's my turn to give back. Don't be afraid to put me to work. Whatever you want done, I'll get right on it. Happy Mother's Day!

35. Here's wishing you a day that brings not only rest and relaxation, but joy, laughter and togetherness. This day is all yours!

36. You devote so much of your time and energy to caring for your family. Today is YOUR day. Enjoy it! You deserve a little rest and relaxation.

37. With every year that passes, you become an even more important part of my life. Nobody could ever replace you, Mom.

38. Being the only parent in the house made it extra hard on you, but that never stopped you from rising to the occasion and being the best parent a person could have. Happy Mother's Day.

39. Mother, 母亲, Madre, Majka, Mor, Móðir, Mam, Moeder. No matter what word you use, it still means love. Happy Mother's Day!

40. Your smile lights the days, your words lift my spirits and your love moves my life. Happy Mother's Day to the most wonderful person in the world.

41. I learned the meaning of happiness from you. You've been such a great teacher and an unbelieveable Mom. Happy Mother's Day!

42. You watched over us during the hard times, the lean times and the sad times, and you made

them all seem a little bit brighter. Happy Mother's Day to a mom who does the impossible all the time.

43. No matter where I go and what I do, you are always there with me. Mom, your love makes me complete and I only wish I could show you how much it means.

44. Now that I'm a mom too, I know how hard it is to smile all the time, but you always did it so naturally. You're a model for all moms. Happy Mother's Day!

45. Whenever I need a hug, I only have to think of you. You're the best and you make my days shine. Happy Mother's Day!

46. I've got so little to give to someone who has given me so much. Big Hug! Big Kiss! Lots of Love!

47. Moms make every day happy for everyone else, but my Mother's Day wish is a happy day that's all yours. You deserve it!

48. You're the person who taught me to look for the good in everyone. That's what a great mother gives the world. Happy Mother's Day!

49. Mothers are all special people, but you stand high above the crowd. I love you so much!

50. A mother's kindness is a seed that blossoms in the garden of her children's hearts. Thank you for teaching me caring, sharing and love.

51. If I could trade places with you, I would try to take on all the things you so unselfishly do, but I doubt I could keep up. I'm not perfect. You are. I love you, mom. Happy Mother's Day!

52. I don't say it enough, but I love you. Thanks for all everything you so unselfishly do for me. You deserve more than just one day's celebration.

53. On this day devoted to you, I hope all the love you've shared comes back to you tenfold. Happy Mother's Day!

54. I have a wonderful life, and I owe it all to you. You've provided my foundation and the roof

over my head. Thank you for everything. Happy Mother's Day!

55. I really don't know what I would do without, Mom. You've made even the most challenging moments of my life a little bit easier. Thank you and Happy Mother's Day!

56. You taught me to care about others by caring for others yourself. You taught me generosity by sharing everything you have. And you taught me to be a good mother by setting a wonderful example when I was young. Thank you for the many gifts you've given me over the years.

57. Even though we can't see each other as often as we'd like, I want to wish you a glorious Mother's Day.

58. May your heart be filled with every joy you've brought me throughout my life. Happy Mother's Day!

59. There are no words to describe a mother like you. I don't know how so much love, compassion, sacrifice, warmth, joy, energy and

life could be wrapped up in one person. But there you are. Happy Mother's Day!

60. There's no such thing as a perfect parent. I know you sometimes wonder if you should have done things differently or been a "better mom," but I want you to know you did just fine raising me. Holding grudges would only hurt the relationship we're establishing now. I really am glad to have you in my life, Mom.

61. There's nothing more special than the love between a mother and a child. No one else in this world has ever been there for me way you have. Heartfelt Thanks and Happy Mother's Day!

62. We haven't been able to see each other much lately, but I think we both know that circumstances beyond our control are keeping us apart. If I had one wish, it would be to spend Mother's Day together. I love you and I miss you, Mom.

63. It wasn't until I became a parent that I realized how many sacrifices you made for me when I

was young. Sorry if I didn't realize it at the time, but I want you to know I get it now. Thank you!

SPECIFIC TO STEPMOMS
AND OTHER FAMILY ARRANGEMENTS

64. You haven't been my mom forever, but I look forward to getting to know you better in the years ahead.

65. It seems like only yesterday that I was acting like a total brat and saying you could never replace my "real mom." Since then, you've shown me that a real mom is one who shows she cares on a daily basis, in word, thought and action. It's sure been a rocky road, but I want to thank you for being a real mom to me.

66. To a grandmother who's always been like a mother to me: I truly appreciate all the time and effort you've devoted to raising me right. Thank you and Happy Mother's Day!

67. A friend and mentor is a rare treasure. Thank you for filling my life with purpose and direction.

68. When I married into your family I knew I was getting something special, but I never could

have prepared myself for how welcome I'd feel. Thanks for making your house feel like home. Happy Mother's Day to a truly amazing mother-in-law!

69. Thank you for bringing the joys of family to me. I feel very privileged to have you in my life. No one else will ever compare!

70. I know what it's like to be a mother, but I will never live up to the standard of perfection you set. You are the best!

71. When I think MOTHER, I think YOU. Thanks for always being there.

72. They say blood is thicker than water, but if there's one thing you've proven it's that love is thicker than blood. Happy Mother's Day, from the bottom of my heart, to the woman who raised me.

73. I haven't always been the perfect child, but you've always been an outstanding parent. Thanks for being strong when I was weak.

74. What could be better than one great mom? Two great moms, of course! Thanks for all the love

and support you both show me throughout the year. Happy Mother's Day!

75. Every so often, a special person walks into your life. After that, you wonder how you ever could have lived without them. Thank you for being the mother figure I've always needed.

76. Mom, no matter where we are on the planet, whether we are liberated or captive, in our hearts we will always be free. Happy Mother's Day to you.

77. I used to get upset when you said no, but now I see it was all about love. Thank you for being the strong, resolute, determined woman you are. I am better for it. Happy Mother's Day from someone who loves you as unconditionally as you've always loved me.

78. A lot of people complain about their in-laws, but not me. Not ever. I'm one of the lucky ones. I've got a mother-in-law who treats me like I'm one of her own. Happy Mother's Day!

79. Happy Mother's Day to a grandma who's about so much more than milk and cookies!

80. Of all the special people in my life, there could never be anyone more special than you. Thanks for teaching me to let love in. Once you start, it's impossible to stop. Happy Mother's Day!

FUNNY AND FUN

81. Remember when I was a kid? Yeah, me neither. That was a million years ago. Man, are we getting old. Anyway, Happy Mother's Day!

82. I don't want to get all sappy on you, Mom. That's just not who we are. Instead, I'll thank you for everything you do while I madly raid your refrigerator. You weren't going to eat this cheese, were you?

83. Some people don't understand why I still live at home, but if they had a mom as amazing as you, they'd all live at home too. I will always be your loving and eternally grateful freeloader!

84. Happy Mother's Day to a mom who ain't no 1950's housewife. What you lack in cooking and cleaning skills, you more than make up for in awesomeness!

85. Sending you my love through the mail. Hope it gets there in one piece (and on time). Happy Mother's Day!

86. Mother's Day is the perfect opportunity to treat yourself to something scrumptious. Have some chocolate. Have some cake. Treat yourself to everything yummy. It's your day. Enjoy it!

87. My friend + my confident + my comfort = my mom. Happy Mother's Day!

88. I don't want to get cheesy about it, but I appreciate all the funny faces you make, all the jokes you crack and all the love you give. You're the best. Happy Mother's Day!

89. They say I've got a face only a mother could love. Well, you've loved this adorable mug through thick and thin, and I want you to know that the feeling is mutual. Thanks for being there, Mom!

90. I know I was a little hell-raiser when I was younger. Oh, who am I kidding? I'm still a hell-raiser now! Thanks for putting up with me. Happy Mother's Day!

91. I thought about treating us to a mani-pedi, then I thought about treating us to a man... and from there it just got weird. Anyway, Happy

Mother's Day. And may we never speak of this awkward card again.

92. The term "World's Greatest Mom" gets brandied about a lot these days, but everybody around here knows the title is yours. Have a good one—you deserve it!

93. Growing up, all my friends were so jealous of me because I had the cool mom. What they didn't know is that I was always envious of you. You really are too cool for school!

94. You are the most important person in the world to me... and not just because you're letting me live in your house rent-free! (You're a pretty great mom.)

95. Give me an M, give me an O, give me a T, give me an H, give me an E, give me an R and what do you have? The very best thing in the world: YOU as my MOTHER. Happy Mother's Day!

96. Is there anything you could do to make yourself a better mom? Nah, of course not! Well... maybe get a tattoo. That would be pretty cool. Happy Mother's Day!

97. Warmth + Understanding + Sacrifice + Love = Mom. See? I told you I did my math homework.

98. Happy Mother's Day!!! For me, it's a 365 day celebration... except for leap years, when it's 366 days. I love you, Mom!

99. Happy Happy Happy Happy Happy Happy Happy Mother's Day. Now aren't you glad I never totally lost that stutter?

100. Even S'mores can't hold a candle to my mom. She's the best treat in the world.   Happy Mother's Day!

101. I didn't bring a gift, but I did bring my laundry. Happy Mother's Day!

101 Sympathy Sentiments for Greeting Cards

Sympathy cards are hard. If you write the wrong thing, you run the risk of making the recipient feel even worse! If you freeze up every time you need to write something in a sympathy card, you are not alone. But what can you do to ensure your inscription is thoughtful and encouraging?

Consult this book!

It contains 101 unique sentiments you can write in sympathy cards for friends, family members, or co-workers. You'll find everything from brief sentiments to personal expressions from the heart. It also includes specialized wishes of hope for those who have lost a dear pet. If someone in your life has lost a loved one and you just can't seem to find the right words, it's time to grab a copy of this ebook!

Kick your fear of "Blank Inside" cards to the curb. Or put your artistic skills to use and make your own! No need to worry about what you'll write inside.

You can provide thoughtful sentiments of sympathy with "What Should I Write? 101 Sympathy Sentiments for Greeting Cards."

Note: In many of these sentiments, [loved one] appears and should be replaced by the name of the person who has passed. Similarly [them/their/they] appears as a gender-neutral pronoun which can be switched out for the pronoun that individual used.

BRIEF SENTIMENTS

1. I'm so sorry for your loss. Please let me know if there's anything I can do.

2. My thoughts are with you and your family in this time of sorrow.

3. May peace fill your heart as you call to mind the wonderful times you and your loved one shared.

4. Those who give love freely live forever in the hearts of we who are left behind.

5. Wishing you hope and support in this time of loss.

6. May the flowers of yesterday fragrance every tomorrow.

7. Your friends are here with love and support in this time of painful loss.

8. Every time we remember the good times spent with the ones we've lost, we keep them alive in our hearts. My deepest sympathies at this difficult time.

9. You will get through this. I know you will. Have faith in your strength.

10. These are dark waters you're navigating. May you be guided by the light of stars above.

11. You are one of the strongest people I know. You will get through this with the care and support of everyone who loves you.

12. Thinking of you during these difficult days.

13. You are not alone. A great many people care about you, and we will remain at your side for as long as you need us.

14. My deepest sympathies as you navigate grief's difficult terrain.

15. I offer my strength and support as you work through the many emotions brought on by this terrible loss.

16. May your faith guide you through these sorrowful days.

17. Even though the ones we've lost seem far away, their memories live forever in our hearts.

18. Extending my deepest, most heartfelt sympathy at this time of loss.

19. Any time you need to talk, I'm only a phone call away.

20. Everyone at the office was truly saddened to hear of your loss. Our thoughts are with you and your family in this time of grief.

21. Wishing you strength and hope.

22. Please accept my most heartfelt condolences.

23. With thoughts of hope and comfort, we send our most heartfelt sympathy.

24. May your faith sustain you as you navigate the difficult days ahead.

25. Thinking of you with sympathy and solace.

26. We're holding you in our hearts at this difficult time

27. Warmest hugs to you and the family.

28. May the care and support of your friends lift you up at this sad time.

29. Our whole family sends its love.

30. Thinking of you and remembering all the wonderful times.

31. Please accept my condolences and know that [loved one] will live on in our minds and hearts.

32. My thoughts are with you and the family.

33. Anyone as special as [loved one] can never be forgotten.

34. May the love of your inner circle guide you through these difficult days.

35. With thoughts of friendship, I offer my shoulder to cry on.

36. Wishing I could hold your hand at this time of loss. Sorry to be so far away.

37. May you find comfort in friendship at this time of loss.

38. Thinking of you with hope that you can feel the warm waves of comfort I'm sending your way.

39. You are not alone. We are here for you. Whatever you need.

40. Words cannot heal your pain, but love can. Please know that you are loved, and that we share in your sorrow.

HEARTFELT SENTIMENTS

41. Nothing can ever replace the loved one you've lost, but I can assure you that, in time, the memories you shared will fill the place in your heart that feels so empty now.

42. I know it feels like the world is closing in and life will never be the same again, and part of that is true. Life won't ever be the same without the one you've lost. But life will go on, and I promise you'll be okay in time. Until then, feel free to rely on me. I'm happy to listen any time you need to talk.

43. There's nothing in life that hurts quite as much as losing someone we love. It's a walk through hell, but when we come out the other side, we emerge with a greater appreciation of everything that remains.

44. Even when those we hold dear have departed this earth, the seeds of love they planted in our hearts continue to flourish and bloom. We are the legacy they leave behind.

45. How can we move forward after the loss of a loved one? How can we even imagine what that looks like when we're so caught up in grief? Well, maybe we can't see the light at the end of the tunnel—not right away. But we need to trust that it's there. We will feel its warmth shining down on us when we're ready.

46. If any good can come out of this time of senseless loss, may it be the realization that your friends, your family, and everyone in your life are here to support you now and for as long as you need our help.

47. You've probably heard of the five stages of grief: denial, anger, bargaining, depression, and acceptance. Whether you experience these emotions in this or any order, I want you to know I'm right here offering support. Any time you need to talk, I'm just a phone call away.

48. There is sorrow now, but in time the pain will turn to peace. The grief will become gratitude that you shared a life with someone so dear. My deepest sympathy.

49. I realize we haven't been on the best of terms lately, but I want to set our differences aside to let you know how sorry I am for your loss. With deepest sympathy.

50. The people in our lives may leave, but love is never lost. It lives forever in our hearts. May thoughts of your time together ease your sorrow and bring you comfort and peace.

51. Whenever you feel weak, I want you to remember your friends are here to offer you strength. We love you, we care, and we're here with support. Anything you need, feel free to ask. We're here for you.

52. Healing begins not when we're blocking out the light, but when we step into the sunshine. We all need time to hide beneath the covers. There's nothing wrong with that. But the time will come to emerge, though we be tattered and frail from tears. That's when the heart finds its strength.

53. If anything can help to ease the ache of loss, may it be the knowledge that your friends are

here to comfort you. With sympathy and support.

54. There's nothing I can say to lessen your pain, but I know you'll get through this. If you need a shoulder to cry on or just someone to reminisce with, you know I'll be there.

55. What a caring, kind, generous person your [mother/father] was. The apple doesn't fall far from the tree! [Their] loving spirit lives on in you.

56. We will never forget the many ways in which [loved one] changed our lives. [Their] absence will be deeply felt.

57. Wishing you islands of comfort and tranquility within the whirlwind of activity that follows the loss of someone so dear. Our thoughts are with you.

58. When one person impacts so many others in such a positive way, you know they lived life right. [Loved one] was a special someone to our whole family. [They] will be sorely missed.

59. Even following a lengthy illness, it's hard to prepare yourself for a loss like this. It's like a part of yourself dies with them. But I know you. You will fill that empty space with memories. You will live in the light of that special love you shared.

60. It's difficult to know what to say at a time like this. I know you hadn't been close with [loved one] in a long time, and maybe you feel weird or guilty about that. You took control of your life and did what you needed for YOU. There's nothing wrong with that. But I realize it's a complicated situation, so please feel free to talk to me about it. I'm on your side.

61. There are sad seasons in life, and this is certainly one of them. But, like the seasons, emotions change over time. One day the rain that seems to shroud your days will encourage loving memories to blossom.

62. You're not alone in all this. It's confusing, it's stressful, it's sad beyond belief. I know. Everyone grieves differently, but take it from

someone who's been knocked down and hit hard: you will get through this. You're not alone.

AS TIME GOES BY

63. It's hard to believe a year has gone by since we lost [loved one]. I still think about [them] all the time. [Loved one] was such a great person—and so are you. I'm so glad to have you in my life. Warmest hugs.

64. I'm so sorry I wasn't able to be there for the service. You've been in my thoughts since I heard the news. Please let me know if there's anything I can do. My deepest condolences to you and the family.

65. This Christmas will be the first without [loved one]. Things sure won't be the same this year, but I know we'll find a way to celebrate her memory. By carrying on her traditions, we'll keep her with us in spirit.

66. I know we're coming up on your first anniversary without [spouse/parent/loved one]. Just thought I'd check in and say I hope you're doing okay.

67. Sending a few words to commemorate [loved one's] birthday. We always used to get together to celebrate, and I think we still should. This year, we'll honour his memory.

68. A year has gone by since [loved one] passed. I don't always mention it, but I hope you're doing okay. My sympathy stays with you. If you ever need to talk, I'm still here.

69. Even after all these years, we still miss [loved one] greatly, as I know you do. Our deepest condolences.

70. Remembering a life so dear. Remembering the love you shared. Sending our sympathy on the anniversary of [loved one]'s passing.

71. It's funny how, once that special someone has died, nothing's ever the same again. Normal never returns. But there's a new normal. Life will never be what it was, but when you've got family and friends who care about you, it's possible to thrive. I see that in you.

LOSS OF PET

72. There is nothing in this world like a devoted friend. I know your pet meant the world to you. I'm so sorry for your loss.

73. A pet is so much more than just an animal that shares your space. A pet is a constant companion. I can only imagine what you must be going through right now. My thoughts are with you.

74. The grief process is different for everyone, but there's no difference between how we feel when we lose a human loved one and how we feel when a beloved pet dies. I want you to know I understand what you're going through and I'm here to offer my support.

75. Some people just don't get it. They make jokes about those of us who feel a deep connection with our pets. But I know from experience what it's like when your best friend dies, and it's no laughing matter. I take your loss seriously, and I'm always here to help.

76. Remember how your fur baby could always cheer you up, no how dark the future looked? It's a dark time indeed when you lose a beloved pet, but I hope one day you'll be able to look back on the fun you shared… and smile.

77. Can there be a more special gift than a devoted companion? At times, it seems like pets can read our minds. By instinct, they know us better than the humans in our lives. A friend like that will always hold a place in our hearts. My deepest sympathy.

78. Our animals never want us to feel sad. May thoughts of your faithful friend sustain you throughout this time of loss.

79. It was impossible to miss the special connection you shared with your pet. I can only imagine how tough this time must be. I'm truly sorry for your loss.

80. Remembering your beloved pet and wishing you solace at this difficult time. Warmest hugs to you and the family.

81. Pets are only with us for a short time, but they change our lives forever. Thinking of you at this time of loss.

82. As you celebrate your dear pet's life, I want you to know how much joy she brought us. She will be truly missed.

83. We're all going to miss your darling dog. Please accept our deepest condolences.

84. Your pet's joyful spirit always put a smile on my face. I'm so sorry for your loss.

85. My deepest sympathy on the loss of a loving companion.

86. We share our condolences as you mourn the loss of such a devoted pet.

87. The way your dear dog gazed up at you, it was like love at first sight every time. That's what pets give us that humans never can: that true, undying affection. And it doesn't go away just because the pet is gone. That love is real. It never dies.

88. They say you can tell a lot about the owner by the temperament of the pet. Your dearly

departed was one of the sweetest and most devoted fur babies I've ever seen—not to mention fun to be around! So it must be true. [They] got that from you.

VERY BRIEF CLOSING SENTIMENTS

89. Warmest Hugs,

90. Deepest Sympathy,

91. With Loving Memories,

92. Keeping you in my thoughts,

93. Heartfelt Condolences,

94. Sincere Condolences,

95. My Condolences,

96. Love and Sympathy,

97. With thoughts of peace,

98. With healing thoughts,

99. With care at this difficult time,

100. With Sympathy and Solace,

101. My thoughts are with you,

For news on upcoming additions to the
"What Should I Write?" series, visit:
http://whatshouldiwriteonthiscard.wordpress.com/

Best Wishes,
Maddie Mayfair

"For all those moments when you can't figure out what
to write in a greeting card…"

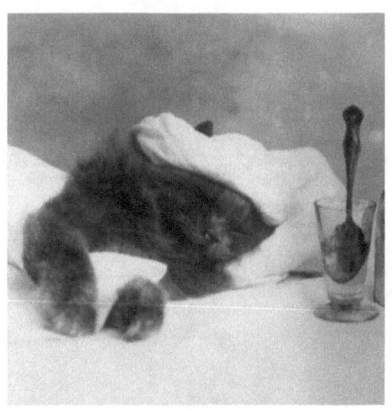

You might also enjoy Crazy Cat Stuff:

https://crazycatstuff.wordpress.com/

Oddities and Commodities Inspired by Cats!